ANOTHER ROSE THAT GREW

FROM CONCRETE

# INTRODUCTION

This is a story about a young man

who grew up in the ghetto and

was surrounded by hate, greed,

crime, filth and poverty. He also

suffered from being bullied by kids

that knew no better, which made

him the underdog in the world that

he live in. He was spat on,

laughed at, teased and abused all

because he happened to be at the

wrong place and time or should I

say he looked different from

everybody around him or because

his skin color was the minority in

the place that he lived. But he still

had faith to be successful and

achieve the goals that he set

before him. So take a look through

his journey to see whether he lived

or died, whether he ended up

happy or sad but just know that

this young one named Rose

happens to be another rose that

grew from concrete.

Inspired by Tupac Shakur

Written  by Jerry

Ayers

Rose was born May 14 2013 on the nicest most beautiful day of the year. The weather was a perfect 77 degrees with no wind. The sky was clear light blue with few rain clouds but there were no rain and the sun was sitting up in the corner shining down on the busy earth. Rose was premature and had a discoloration effect due to the mass pollution in the air.

Rose was born in the harsh ghetto

in the state of New Jersey that

was named one of the top ten

dirtiest states in the United States

and one of the top ten states with

the highest crime rates and

murder rates and one of the most

states with the highest pollution in

the air because almost all new

Jerseyians smoked tobacco and

Mary Jane or weed. Plus many

people drove so the gas in the

cars burned up into pollution which

increased the sickness in the air.

But It was not Rose fault that he

was born to this environment but

as Rose got older and used to the

piece of earth he was living at and

because he felt like since his

name is Rose, he deserved a

better location more like a real

garden because he wondered why

New Jersey was called the garden
state where there were hardly any
gardens. All he saw was chopped
down trees, junk yards and
starving grasses across New
Jersey. So he wish he was born in
Florida or Hawaii or some other
place but then he realize he was
stuck in the hell hole, plus he was
all alone because when he was
born his mother died giving birth

known to the reason that she

suffered from cancer. Luckily the

cancer didn't transmit to Rose

because he would have died

quicker than his mother did

because the cancer effect would

have been too powerful or strong

for him at a young age.

Rose parents also grew up in the

same place where he was born at

but his parents had it much better

than him because in the 90s there

were more food and less poverty,

and plus the water tasted better

because it was more pure. But

now today the water they drink is

fixed with chemicals and so called

vitamins and contains a lot of lead.

But anyway Rose parents had

another child before him and her

name was Rosey but she was

kidnapped on the very day she

was born in April 14 2010. While

Rose parents dozed off after the

birth of Rosey, Rosey was

snatched by a mature short dark

skinned lady with dreads that

wears glasses who came to visit

New Jersey from Atlanta Georgia.

Rose mother and father were very

upset that their daughter Rosey

has gone missing and still today

there are no finds of her. And it

was difficult searching for Rosey

because April was a rainy month

that rained 22 days out of 31 and

plus it had some of the foggiest

days of the year. So they decided

to have another child in the

coming year because they were

getting too old so they wanted to

strengthen their roots and

increase their family tree. But they

had to make sure they keep one

eye open in the city of thieves and

kidnappers to make sure the same

thing doesn't happen to their next

child. But unfortunately in the year

of 2013 Rose mother developed

skin cancer and his father

disappeared and was last seen in

April 2013.

By July, the first day of summer,

Rose pigmentation was finally

recovering and started to appear

attractive. He had a light reddish

silky skin color that'll attract any

beautiful women that walks pass

him if they noticed him because he

was very small and still growing.

Like how some people dance for

money, Rose was a thirsty fella

that would dance back and forth

all day especially on the windy

days in hopes someone give him a

bottle of water or even a few drops

would of helped in the summer's

hottest days. One day it was so

hot like 99 degrees, Rose decided

to take a day off from dancing

because he didn't want to look

suspicious by dancing in the heat

so when he got thirsty he prayed

for it to rain to at least have some

water going in his body; so that he

don't become dehydrated and dry

out and become old. But luckily

later that day it went from 99

degrees to 80 degrees and it

started to drizzle so he was able to

cool off. Sadly for the next three

days it rained non-stop and it was

like karma for him because he

prayed for it to rain before and

now he's suffering because he's

getting more than he asked for.

And since he don't have a home

and nobody to take care of him, he

got soaked from too much water

and became so sick that he

couldn't stand up straight anymore

and was feeling down for the next

four days. After a while Rose

started to feel a lot better and

started to straighten back up and

active like he once was. Then by

August he grew tired of his

loneliness and wondered about his

father and sister he was told

about. He knew his mother died

but he still wanted to know the

history of his family roots, so he

set a goal for himself that when he

get older he will do some

searching.

As Rose got older, taller and

stronger, people started to notice

him and he enjoyed that until he

learned that popularity has a

downside and when you stand out,

people will try to pick you apart.

And when you're different, people

will stare at you like they never

seen anything like you before. And

some are rude and will try to kick

you out of place. But Rose already

felt out of place and wanted to go

to a place where he would be

considered a majority, and where

everyone looks like him instead of

looking at him. He liked the

attention at first until one day he

saw a bunch of little bad kids

coming and when they saw him

they all pointed and laughed at

him. Also one of the kids had

poured a bottle of soda on him

because he looked thirsty. But

Rose sucked it up because he

didn't let anything bother him.

Every time he see those kids

walking his way he'll do his best to

look away or try to hide under a

rock or something. But Rose loved

insects but not all of them

especially black flies because they

seemed to be everywhere and

they're dirty because they always

around the garbage. One thing

Rose hated about blackflies or

house flies, is that they be eating

feces and then come around

spreading germs by touching. But

Rose liked bees because they

seem nice to him and never stings

him. Rose also loved butterflies

but he never got a chance to see

one up close because where he

lives they will die by being crushed

by ant bullies and other monsters

that walks by.

As fall was approaching and

summer was nearly over, Rose

started to feel the chills of the

unpleasant breeze and wish that

he had something like him to

cuddle up with. But in the area that

he stayed at, he saw no one that

he liked because there were not

many of his kind that lived in New

Jersey. The only time he saw his

kind was on every other Sunday

where a lot of cars tailgating each

other where two police cars or

motorcycles in front of a long car.

They were pretty but they were too

old for him, so his luck was slim in

finding the right one for him. As fall

was penetrating, Rose began to

feel uncomfortable as solitary

infected him and made him look

old, crumbled and weary. He was

still young but he just needed a

warm home to maintain his young

look before people starts to really

mistreat him. The place he was

living at was cold because it had

no windows, it was dangerous

because too many people passed

by, kids were rude and people

bumped you without saying

excuse me but there was nothing

Rose could do anything about it

because he was small and red in a

tall black and white man world. As

time went by, fall was deep in its

season. Fog showed up on car

windows, ice appeared on the

roads and air became visible

every time somebody took a

breath. The only thing Rose liked

about the cold fall was that less

people were outside, he knew that

the less people that's walking

around the less likely he'll get

pushed around or kicked in the

face. Just because he's a midget

to people, he has been kicked

around, laughed at, stared at, and

sometimes there were people that

took pictures of him just to show

off to the world like nature made a

mistake somewhere. But it was

nature itself that chose him to be

the odd one out.

On the first day of winter it got

worst. It was late December and

snowflakes begin to fall. Still

without a warm home, Rose was
struggling to survive in the cold air.
He knew that in a few weeks he
would wear and tear and die of
sickness from the cold. And that's
when he hated New Jersey even
more and begin to feel Florida was
where he belongs. And he felt like
if he don't make it there soon, he
will die from the cold but he knew
that nobody cared about him or

wondered how he felt being all

alone because people just walked

by seeing this poor fellow

shivering and just pointed at him

and kept on walking. But luckily

this short dark skinned mature

lady with dreads that wears

glasses came out of a hummer

and saw this poor fellow dying

between the rocks and pulled

Rose out of the crack of the

concrete and got in her car and

drove off to Atlanta. Then she

placed Rose in the Peace Garden

of Tupac Shakur and that's when

he saw his sister Rosey for the

first time. And Rose and Rosey

bunched together and lived happy

ever after.

# A Poem dedication to Tupac

One thing I regret about Tupac, is
that I didn't get a chance to meet
him/ Oh I wish I had a chance to
meet him, greet him and show
peace to him because he inspired
my thoughts, he kept feeding
them/ Sadly some people say his
name in vain/ But they don't know
that every time they say his name
they give him more fame/ The
swear he wasn't loyal to the game
but they just mad because he

inspired millions to make a
change/ I don't know if I can
change the world but I do know he
sparked my brain/ Some say it's
idol worship but if they would
recognize a person that's sent
from God, they would do the
same/ Instead the media only
show the bad side of him looking
strange/ But if they ever met
Tupac they would have something
to treasure down their memory
lane/ Even after 17 years haters

still spitting on his grave/ I guess
they still mad because he
unchained the slaves that made
the brain free in the hip hop
community because he was brave/
Now since the 90s died with him
hip hop started using gays and he
warned us about this in his last
days to prevent many from going
to their graves/ Some say he was
trying to be a gangster and trying
to Bishop/ But they fail to realize
that he always had that personality

and wisdom/ In "Juice" he was just being himself showing his "Don't give a fuck attitude" But haters say he was trying to be somebody else but all I saw was him wearing his own shoes/ It's funny they never mention his kindness in "Poetic Justice" they just keep talking how he changed after "Juice" But their IQ is too low to understand that Bishop was really you(2pac)/ They just want to discredit his fame and throw dirt on his name because they just jealous of him/ lol, they thought they killed him but they didn't because he is still relevant/ He will always be alive through my poetry because my writings birthed from his intelligence/ If he was alive today he will get my vote to be president because I trust his leadership and his common sense/ The people that never understood him obviously never had common sense/ They just saw him with one eye, heard him with one ear, reached out to him with one hand, thought of him for a few seconds is the reason they're ignorant/ But to me I saw him on TV with two eyes, heard him on CD with two ears, reached out to him with both hands; is the reason why I'm so intelligent/ People are mentally poor because they speak without paying attention/ Since 2pacalypse they couldn't wait for Armageddon because they don't want the truth to get to the masses so they censor his thoughts so it can only be Strictly 4 Niggaz/ So I understand why he sent the message through a Thug Life form so they wouldn't recognize that he was Against The World to save the world from growing devils horns/ Even in his death he still got All Eyez on him because his realness gave him the everlasting mourn/ It's going on 2014 and every memorial he become reborn inside the hearts that was torn/ It's like people keeping him alive to keep their smiling turning into a frown/ So they pass on the 7 Day Theory to prove he aint in the ground/ But if he is or not I always will remember him because I am still down/ Don't matter how many lies they make about him, I'm still by his side/ The media only show his reactions without the cause but still he rise/ He never will die, his words will live forever because the truth will never hide/ A lot of

people hate him because he was
wise/ No blasphemy but I would of
thought he was Christ if I was
blind/ Not saying that Jesus was
white, we all know that's a lie and
sadly they'll continue that white lie
Until The End Of Time/ But I'm still
praying for Better Dayz but the
dark nights still taking its time/ And
if I die fighting a triangle with one
eye then I'm sure Jehovah will
forgive me with both eyes and
plan a resurrection for me with

greater lives/ If it wasn't for Pac I wouldn't know how to endure the pain because of him I have been Loyal To The Game/ It was Pac's Life that kept me out of chains/ If I would of never heard Keep Ya Head Up I probably would of made a race of babies and hated the ladies/ If I never would of heard Dear Mama I would never had thought of her as a queen, just a nicotine fiend that be going crazy/ I kept a condom on since Brenda

Had A Baby and if I never heard "Smile" I would of kept a frown and act shady/ And since I read the "Rose That Grew From Concrete" I been trying to grow out of the projects of suffering poverty/ If I never would of heard of Thugz Mansion I would of held that nine without thinking about my mother losing her baby/ See it was Pac voice that woke me up and if I never paid attention I would probably be a goner/ If I aint Stare

Through My Rearview I would of saw Death Around The Corner/ I was a Shorty That wanted to be a Thug but that was former/ I wish he can Picture Me Rolling because it was his influence that I made Changes/ My Life Goes on now I'm no longer banging/ Since the Good Die Young I'm going to keep praying/ Your words is like air, it keeps me Breathing in a world of Satan but your Unconditional Love made me hold on when I'm Trapped in

Temptations/

The ignorant say he weren't lyrical

because he didn't use a punch line

or metaphor/ So I ask them to

define lyricism, is it long words

that shares the same meaning of

short letter words like war/ Does it

has to be a famous quote or

philosophy from somebody else or

just yours/ Well I think lyricism is

something that open up the brain

doors/ Lyricism is something that

makes you rock your head back and forth with sweat coming out of your facial pores/ Lyricism is censored because it threatens the laws and have presidents talking about your words and taking you to court/ But the ignorant still believes that lyricism makes them laugh and fall on the floor/ No true lyricism sacrifice itself for its people and prepares to go to courts/ True lyricism makes foreheads sweat and tears fall/

True lyricism makes you forget

that a beat is there and its words

hijacked your thoughts/ and that's

why Pac was the greatest lyricist

because even the haters and the

ones who claim they don't listen to

him; have his words stuck in their

thoughts/

Tupac is the new definition of legend because of the work he did in only 25 years/ Not because he's most famous for his rap career or because he was a gifted actor and a poet, it's because he really cared/ Pac will be the biggest influence on modern hip hop for many years because his innovative lyrics is still relevant, important and reflective that brings happiness and tears/ Started as a back-up dancer and a roadie to an

Iconic figure that affected

everybody rap career/ And when

he started to blow, the devil

started to show/ 5 gunshots

paused his tracks but he

continued his flow/ Accusations

and lawsuits tried to darken his

shine but he kept that window

closed/ Even when he was a

caged bird he could of got bailed

out by Interscope/ He made them

20 million and they still let go of

the rope/ They was hoping he die

in there so they can keep his gross/ But God put his hand on his brain and let him continue to grow/ And since then he became the greatest song writer that we ever know/ The emotion the feeling the honesty and the passion in his songs made us believe in hope/

Honesty I would of took a bullet for Pac even if It was Gang Related/ Because I saw Above the Rim how he was educating/ Some say he was Nothing But Trouble but I

say his anger was just Poetic
Justice because criminal justice
wasn't doing their job and being
racist/ Now I understood why he
Gridlock'd and pop at 2 cops in
that situation/ They got shot in the
ass because they were being
assholes so every time they squat,
a thought of their ignorance starts
racing/ But that's what they get for
thinking they had the "Juice" when
karma is the resurrection of abuse,
now they hate to be naked/

If I was young I would be a Pac kid

in the Tupac Amari Shakur

Foundation/ But it aint too late for

my graduation because his history

is responsible for my successful

making/ This book is written just to

help me make a TASF donation/

## Make a Donation

Consider giving a gift that will help us sustain today's youth. Tupac Amaru Shakur is a  public charity that relies on generous donations from the public. Without these generous donations the needs of our charity would likely go unmet. There are many charities that are hard at work meeting the existing needs in our world and creating a better life for those they serve. We pray that you will choose this charity for your year-end tax deductible donation.

Over the last 15 years we have provided a safe haven for youth from all backgrounds to freely express themselves through the arts in a positive environment. A contribution you make, in any size, will help support another year of leadership & arts programs for youth who aspire to enhance their creative talents, and youth who have never had any formal training in the arts. Every dollar counts. Your support will help us spend the next 12 months building children's team work/collaboration skills, presentation skills, public speaking, self-confidence, conflict resolution, and values through the arts. The arts are a good place for grief, and non-injurious way to deal with pain. The arts can open students up to greater academic achievement and increase self-esteem.

We believe the greatest investment one can make is in the life of a child. There's still time! Make your year-end tax deductible donation to the Tupac Amaru Shakur Foundation. Your investment will help fund a full year of afterschool enrichment classes, leadership & arts summer camps, youth mentoring, garden projects, youth scholarships, food pantry, and a community art center and 6-acre garden that annually attracts hundreds of visitors from around the world.

Tupac strived to reach out and help as many people as he could. We thank our donors and Tupac's fans that have supported us in the past! You have helped fuel a necessary work in our communities. We're depending on your continued support. The help, not hate, that young people need in this world does not end. As long as that need exist, a legacy of encouragement, education, and opportunity must continue.

What we do now, matters forever!

Peace, Love, and Respect,
Tupac Amaru Shakur Foundation

Send checks or money
orders to:
Tupac Amaru Shakur
Foundation
5616 Memorial Drive
Stone Mountain, Georgia
30083
The Tupac Amaru Shakur
Foundation is a 501c3 public
charity. Tax ID 582512839

## MISSION

Our mission is to provide training and support for students who aspire to enhance their creative talents. Each and every child desires freedom to creatively express themselves. We provide an environment that encourages freedom of expression, serves as a resource for families, and empowers via education.

# ABOUT

The Tupac Amaru Shakur Foundation (TASF) is home to the Tupac Amaru Shakur Center for the Arts, just outside of Atlanta in Stone Mountain, Georgia. TASF was founded in 1997 originally as the Shakur Family Foundation by Afeni Shakur, mother of multi-talented Tupac Amaru Shakur. Since its inception TASF has offered performing arts camps, essay competitions, youth book clubs, visual arts workshops, community development projects, and scholarships to students pursuing undergraduate degrees.

On June 11, 2005 the TASF opened the Center! The Center is dedicated to providing youth and the community with educational programs in the arts. It is a fact that early arts education improves school grades, as well as offers invaluable life lessons while building self-esteem and confidence. For nearly 15 years, the Foundation's programs have served youth of all social and economic backgrounds, giving countless young people the courage to get off the streets and learn vital skills that have the potential to positively impact their communities. The Center is open to the public and hosts several noteworthy events throughout the year.

## MORE ABOUT TUPAC

Tupac Amaru Shakur dealt with great obstacles such as homelessness, hunger, and pain, amongst other situations during his youth. Performing arts provided the hope that would seed the expression that would one day influence generations worldwide.

Tupac accomplished a lot before his murder at the age of 25. At an early age, he wrote and organized family productions, casting himself as the lead and his older cousins in supporting roles. Tupac formally trained at the 127th Street Ensemble and Baltimore School for the Arts. At the age of twelve, he experienced his first formal stage role as the character "Travis" in the stage play 'Raisin In the Sun' at the prestigious Apollo Theatre in Harlem.

Tupac was eventually cast in several feature films and recorded several chart topping albums. In fact, he released the first ever double hip-hop CD.   Today, years after his physical departure, he is the second highest selling Hip-Hop artist of all time. His gift- his words and creative talent- continues to inspire others around the world!

# OTHER BOOKS TO READ

This book here discuss the
real meaning of Nigger, Black,
African, African American
and colored people. The Au-
thor shows the history and
the curse of the N-Word. Un-
like any other book, this book
breaks down the word com-
pletely for this generation and
the younger generation of to-
morrow.

JERRY AYERS

This book here discusses the real
meaning behind the words Nigger,
black, African American and colored
people. Unlike any other book, this
one breaks the word down
completely giving the reader full
understanding of the word.

Similar to "Roots" but this story is a fantasy of what many wish that happened instead. The whites thought that they was profiting off of a slave but later they found out that they captured the wrong slave, the slave that hunted each and every one of them..Horror

Relax and let each poem take you into a different world. You're guaranteed to come back with more wisdom, confidence and appreciation.

A memorial of Black History

Colored Entrance

Black History Month Poems

J A

Poetic Stories

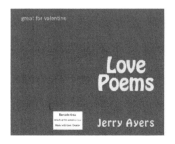

# Beautiful Love Poems

Chanel was a pregnant prostitute who sold her body to support her drug addiction, who twin daughters were separated at birth due to a tragic event that took place. Her daughter's grew up not knowing either one of them existed. They both went through their own struggle in life that brought them together as one...... by Gerald Toatley

Made in the USA
San Bernardino, CA
19 November 2014